Proper Finger Line-Up

Learn to Type

Judith Robbins Barrett
Copyright © 2018 Judith Robbins Barrett
All rights reserved.

INTRODUCTION

Typing is not difficult if you learn the initial finger line-up. As you do the lessons and speed tests, you will go at a very slow pace to let your motor muscles memorize your movements across the keyboard.

Typing is eye to paper (or computer screen) contact. The less you look at the keys, the more accurate you will be in the long run, which is the ultimate goal. It is mere practice.... and at your own pace I might add.

After you have become accustomed to the feel of the keyboard and have mastered a few of the simple exercises, I will increase the difficulty. You will find a blown up copy of the complete chart on the very last page, which you may remove and used separately for your convenience.

When you glance at the chart, avoid looking at the keys. Return directly to the lesson you are typing.   Remember to keep at a slow pace in the beginning.

Lesson #1

Good posture is an absolute must. Sit up straight, shoulders back, and your feet flat on the floor. This will guarantee less back strain and enable you to remain on your typing project for longer periods of time. With your forefingers on [f] and [j], rest your fingers on the keyboard as shown directly below this paragraph and don't forget the semi-colon. I call it the initial finger line-up.

LEFT	RIGHT
a s d f	**j k l ;**

When you are ready to start your first exercise, rest your dominating thumb lightly on the long bar (space bar) on the keyboard. (When you're not spacing between words or sentences, your thumb might float as you type each letter.) Place your fingers on the line up and begin to type the letters in the chart above. Look only at the chart when you are typing. If you loose track of what finger to use, you can easily return to the line-up. Whenever I pause to check a passage or ponder on a particular "something," I automatically rest my fingers over the initial finger line-up.

The letters [F] and [J] have a small raised dot on each of their keys so that you can locate them by feel. Once you've gotten the hang of it and are progressing nicely, your left and right forefingers should automatically gravitate to [F] and [J]. It will become second nature to you.... with minimal awareness.

Maintaining proper line-up and working from left to right, type the letters in the following chart, moving each finger to slightly above-left for [q] and then slightly below-right for [z] and so on. Do these exercises as many times as you need to master the letter locations. Rest your thumb on the space bar and begin. Keep in mind that all keys that extend up or down from the finger line-up will slant up to the left and down to the right.

LEFT-HAND
aqz swx dec frv
RIGHT-HAND
jum ki, lo. ;p/

Now, using the *shift key, not the *Caps-Lock key, type from the same chart using CAPITAL letters. Read on before you do.

It will get a little tricky when doing this. You must press the shift key on the right side of the keyboard to type [AQZ] but will revert to using the shift key on the left side of the keyboard for all the rest.

Using the left shift key and typing a letter on the left side of the finger line-up will be a challenge at first. You must hold the left shift key with your left pinky finger while pressing the letters [SWX] with your left ring finger. Do the same for [DEC] using your left middle finger and [FRV] using your left forefinger. Once you reach the letters on the right side of the finger line-up, you will continue to use the left shift key with your left pinky finger while using your right forefinger for [JUM] - your right middle finger for [KI<] - your right ring finger for [LO>] and your right pinky finger for [:P?].

If you think you're ready, let's go a step further. Extend the left forefinger to type the letters [GTB] and then extend the right forefinger to type the letters [HYN].

LEFT HAND
aqz swx dec frv gtb
RIGHT HAND
hyn jum ki, lo. ;p/

And in capital letters:

LEFT HAND
AQZ SWX DEC FRV GTB
RIGHT HAND
HYN JUM KI< LO> :P?

* Caps-Lock can be used for headings or to emphasize a word or phrase.

Lesson #2

This time you'll attempt a few sentences. Use the shift key to capitalize the first letter of each sentence and the first letter of each proper name. Use the space bar at the bottom of the keyboard to space between the words. Type the following sentences using the chart on the last page.

****

This is fun.
I will be an accomplished typist in no time.
John browsed the Internet for hours before finding what he wanted.
Are we done yet?

****

Lesson #3

The following sentences are longer and have more difficult words.

****

Joe went to the shore to forget, but his mind stayed on her.

The storm spit forth an insanely, fierce lightning and beat the wild thunder like a sonic boom.

It was imperative that the young girl be on time for the interview if she wanted to land the new job at the art gallery.

****

Lesson #4

Now that you are a pro, lets try a paragraph. You will need to double space at the end of each sentence, which you will do by hitting the space bar twice before starting the next sentence. It's as simple as that.

When you come to the end of the paragraph, use the "Enter" key with your right pinky finger to begin a new one. But when typing within each paragraph, you will type continuously, letting the words wrap automatically.

Let's give it a try.

****

Be all you can, and then some, for time is short. Do exactly as you plan. Some people quickly forgets his or her dream with useless time spent. It takes practice to be a whiz.
****

Lesson #5

It's time for some difficulty. Let's tackle the number keys. They sit above the top row of the letter keys. For example, the number [1] sits just above the letter [Q] and slightly to its left.

Rest your fingers on the finger line-up keys. Type the number [1] by extending the finger that rests on the letter [a]. Type the number [2] by extending the finger that rests on the letter [s]. Continue to do this until you reach the number [0]. You will use your left forefinger for both [4] and [5] and the right forefinger for both [6] and [7]. It won't be easy at first, but you love a challenge, right? Sure you do.

****
1 2 3 4 5 6 7 8 9 0
****

Lesson #6

Below are some number exercises for you to tackle. Type the numbers using the chart below and remember, no peeking. Unless you are in need of typing numbers, you can put this one off until you've mastered the letters. It's entirely up to you.

Using the finger position line-up, begin and don't forget to reach, reach, reach.

****

3,111, 7,228, 5,440, 1,000, 3,245, 5,119, 4,667, 5,891, 3,998

****

Lesson #7

The upper case to the number keys is where you'll find the punctuations and symbols. Use the right shift key for [!], which is on the [1] key. Use the left shift key for the rest. You will use your left forefinger for both the [$] and [%] and your right forefinger for both the [^] and [&]. Run through the exercise as many times as you need. Additional punctuations are to the right of the letter and number keys.

****
! @ # $ % ^ & * ( ) - = [ ] \ . _ + { } |
: " < > ?
****

Lesson #8

I will now include sentences that have numerous types of punctuations and symbols. In sentence #9, you will hold down the left shift key as you type the line
****

1) The toys are priced @ $2.00 each.
2) The box weighs 100 #'s [# meaning pounds].
3) We are working on lesson #8.
4) Tom does 50% (that's 1/2) of the workload.
5) 2 + 5 = 7, & 3 - 1 = 2, & 9 - 3 = 6, & 8 - 4= 4
7) Put an * before each referenced item.
9) Sign here:_____

****

Speed Test #1

Now that you have become familiar with all of the keys on the keyboard, it is time to begin the speed-tests. These are not speed-tests in the sense of speed, but are primarily for the purpose of testing your accuracy. Speed is secondary. Do not worry about any errors that occur.... continue typing. This is important because the more words counted in the allotted time the better your score will be. You could fit two, three, or more words to your count in the amount of time you would spend correcting a mistake. In time, with practice, your accuracy will increase.

Set a timer for the allotted time and type the paragraph. Try to maintain a steady stream of typing; don't try to go fast yet. Remember to let the words wrap automatically. If you finish the paragraph before the timer goes off, keep typing. Simply start the paragraph over again. On the other hand, if you don't complete the paragraph before the buzzer, it's ok because you can still count what you've typed.

Stop when the buzzer sounds and go back and count all the words that you have typed correctly. Microsoft Word has a "Word Count" feature, which you could utilize. It can be found in the "Tools" menu. Delete all the errors, highlight what's left, and click on "Word Count." Divide the total by the time allotted to get your word count per minute. If you don't have Microsoft Word or similar software, you can count manually. Once you have become proficient at the keyboard, you can adjust the speed in all the speed test for a more challenging endeavor.

Time: 3 minutes:

****

Now I can type. Steady to the end. It will be better to remember that quality and accuracy are the ultimate goals. Type at an even pace and you will acquire more speed in the long run. Do you want to be a fast and accurate typist? Of course you do! And you will be if you follow all the guidelines that I have given you.

****

Speed Test #2

Time: 5 minutes:

****

The 20th century alone had brought tremendous revolutionary discoveries to our nation and the world. Everything seemed to just bloom - from cars to computers - from architecture to fashion. Judging from the rate of progress in just the past decade, we will probably double in advancement within just the next few years.

Technology will be 2 or 3 times more intense with the use of sophisticated means of research and development that now exists. It will be interesting to see what's next. Will we float to our jobs or beam to high places? It won't be long before we have computerized chefs in the kitchen and time travel in the elevator. When I am in my twilight years, I hope that I will remember how to put on my shoes.

****

Speed Test #3

Time: 5 minutes:

****

We gather around the dinner table to enjoy the anticipated meal. An elaborate display of specialty dishes works its delectable weave of enticement, wetting our appetites as we wait. Stuffed pork, three styles of spicy potatoes, an array of vegetables, fresh fruit salad, and champagne-on-ice adorn the serving bench, teasing our taste buds as we make small talk to pass the time before the last plate is served.

As the night wears on and our quenched appetites are evident in the relaxed glow of soft conversation, a narrow beam of blue light snaps into the room, burning the windowpane in its wake, knocking William out of his chair.

"William!" I shout.

"Everyone get down!" Jack yells as he runs to William's side. "It's too late. He's gone."

"No!" I scream. "What's happening? I thought you destroyed the beacon!"

****

Speed Test #4

Time 10 minutes:

****

"We thought we did, too," said Jack. "There must be another one."

"We have to search the house. It's got to be right here somewhere."

"It's the first place I'd look," Jack agrees. "But we have to stay low until the spaceships are gone."

"Anyone else hit?" I ask, looking around the room.

"Bobby was hit," Melissa whimpers as she wipes the tears from her eyes. "He's gone."

"I'm so sorry, Melissa. Everyone else alright?" I ask.

"We're okay," says David, who is holding Lilly beneath him in an effort to shield her.

"I'm alright," Mr. Mackinsey says, peaking out from behind the bar.

Jack crawls to the nearest window and steals a cautious observation of the spinning ships.

"There are four of them, hovering near the bluff," he reports.

"Jack, you and I can search the house. We're immune to the aliens' weapons. They only want our alien friends."

"We are?" "Let's go then. I'll search down here; you go upstairs and see what you can find up there."

"Got it," and I run up the stairs.

I search every room, every closet, every bathroom, but. there is no beacon anywhere on the second floor.

"There's nothing up here," I yell.

"Nothing down here either," says Jack, who makes an appearance at the bottom of the stairs.

"What should we do?"

"Check the attic," he tells me. I'll check the basement."

"Okay."

I run to the closet where I see the rope that hangs from cut wood that is closed flush with the ceiling in the far corner. When I pull at the rope, I am presented with a ladder that makes its descent to land directly at my feet. I climb up to the dusty, crawl space where I see a blinking light that pulsates in harmony with intermittent beeps. I back-step down the ladder, run to the top of the stairs, and yell to Jack.

"Up here!"

****

Speed Test #5

Time 20 minutes:

****

"He doesn't hear you," yells Mr. Mackinsey. "I'll crawl to the basement door and yell down to him."

Mr. Mackinsey moves with caution, dodging the blue light beams as he goes, reaching the basement door after a considerable amount of effort.

"Jack, come to the stairs," he yells through the doorway.

"I'm not having much luck down here," Jack shouts up to him.

"Amanda found it in the attic," shouts Mr. Mackinsey.

"She found it? That's great. I'm on my way up, now."

Jack climbs the ladder to the attic and crawls along the unfinished flooring to reach the beacon. He smashes it with his feet, thrusting his legs up and down, stomping at it while he teeters in a sitting position on the protruding floor beam.

"Well, that's that," he says to me. "I hope this is the end of it."

Jack and I return to our friends, who are still huddled below the windows on the first floor. The ships have not left the bluff and they continue their rapid assault, sending their killer lights into the room.

"It looks as though they're not going to leave," I say to Jack.

"They do seem to be hanging around a bit longer than they did the last time they paid us a visit," Jack responds. "There must be a way to confront them."

"No one's done that before," offers Mr. Mackinsey.

"Maybe that's to our advantage," says Jack.

"How's that?" I ask.

"Well, if they aren't expecting a rebuttal from us, we might be able to knock them off their guard in our attempt to fight back, giving us the edge," says Jack. "We need to come up with a plan of attack. We must use something that will scare them off."

"But what?" I ask.

"I know what. The people from my planet don't like water," says Melissa. "The chemical makeup of water is not compatible with their molecular structures. The feeling of slime, as they call it, sends them into a frenzied fit and if that were to happen, they would lose control of the ship."

"That's interesting," I remark.

"We can use the hose," says Jack. "We can hook it up to the outside spigot, pull it to the edge of the bluff, turn it on, and spray water at the crafts in hopes that the structures aren't air tight."

"But they'll see you," I say.

"You must be sure that you're not seen," says Jack. "They do have weapons that will hurt you or even kill you."

"I thought they were only out to get people like you," says Jack."

"They are, normally," says Lilly. "They choose not to kill humans, but that doesn't mean that they can't or won't."

"Well, I'll just have to be careful, then, now won't I," says Jack. "Come with me, Amanda. You can help me hook up the hose. The rest of you stay down."

Jack and I approach a side of the house that is hidden from the space ships' view and gather the hose from a small shed that sits alone near the house.

"Attach the hose to that spigot," instructs Jack. "When I yank it, turn it on."

"Be careful, darling!"

"Don't worry, Amanda, I plan to. We're going to finish this once and for all."

Jack drags the hose toward the edge of the bluff. Bent down at the knees, he moves with slow, humping steps, using caution in his steps, staying close to the ground. After directing the hose toward the first ship, he administers a hefty yank, signaling me to turn on the spigot. With a few turns of the handle, the water gushes forth to cover the entire craft, sending it into a mad, awkward spin before it crashes to the bottom of the bluff. He then directs the hose toward the second ship, manifesting the same result.

The two remaining ships flash their strobe lights across the lawn, exposing Jack as he aims the hose at his third target. He obliterates one of them with the water's powerful thrust.

****

Speed Test #6

Time 20 minutes:

****

The lone, surviving space ship shoots an array of pink light-beams, producing damaging flames that burn with a fury to consume the blades of grass. Jack's agility fails him in his attempt to spray the last ship and the ominous beams torch the left legging of his trousers as they whip at the ground around him. The fiery clothing cripples him, dropping him to the ground, and he rolls his body on the lawn in an effort to diminish the devastating burns. Not a whimper is uttered from his mouth.

"Jack!" I scream. "Jack! Answer me!"

I run to him, my clumsy sling slowing me, leaning me to one side, and once I reach a close proximity to his precarious position, the space ship turns its assault on me. As I sprawl on the ground, Jack makes one last effort to gain aim on the ship and the spray of water bursts wide to cover the craft, resolving the last perilous threat into oblivion.

"Jack!. Are you alright, my darling?"

"I don't know," he says and we embrace as we express relief that the assault has ended. "It's my leg. The stinging pain is unbearable but I'll live."

"I must put out the fire, Jack. Hold still while I give it a good soaking."

"Okay."

I spread the solid spray back and forth, holding on for dear life with one arm until nothing but a scorched, black ember cover a patch of grass, dirt and stones. The water extinguishes the flames without an ounce of resistance.

"That's done. Ok, sweetheart, put your arm around my shoulder. Let's get you back to the house."

Are you sure you can hold me, Amanda?"

"We'll know in a minute," I respond as I help him to his feet.

"Did you see the way those ships lost control when I sprayed them?" he asks.

"I sure did! You were just amazing, sweetheart!"

"I know."

Jack's weight is difficult for me to bear. My throbbing arm hinders my every move as I struggle to keep him on his feet. We make our way toward the house. After several set backs, we arrive in the living room where Jack stretches his body on the couch, favoring his injured leg as he lifts it onto the cushions. I cut Jack's clothing from his wound while Melissa calls for the physician.

"That looks nasty," I say to him, my obvious concern hanging on every word.

"Awe, it's nothing. I'm just thankful that this ordeal has finally come to an end. It's a shame that we had to lose two more of our friends."

"Yes, it is," I agree. "It's very upsetting."

"It's very sad, indeed," he says. "What a lousy, needless waste! Tomorrow, we'll search the entire estate for more beacons and destroy them. We want to make sure there's not a single one left lying around, right Mr. Mackinsey."

"Yes, sir," answers Mr. Mackinsey. "But what do you mean by we? You'll be laid up with that leg for quite a while. Let me do it."

"So I will. I appreciate your offer. It's all yours."

"Thank you, Jack. It'll be a pleasure. Besides, it's part of my job now that I'm your new foreman."

"You're quite right," Jack says to him. "I still appreciate it, though."

"How do you feel, darling?"

"I'm okay, Amanda. The pain seems to have subsided a bit."

"I'm going to wait on you hand and foot, sweetheart. You'll want for nothing, you'll see."

"Have I told you lately just how wonderful I think you are?"

"Let me see," I say with a grin.

"Don't be coy with me," Jack says with a smile. "It

will get you everywhere. There's no doubt in my mind that I've chosen the girl of my dreams," Jack says. "Only...."

"Only what, darling?"

"Only, I wish I had known it sooner."

LEFT   RIGHT
! @ # $ %   ^ & * ( )
1 2 3 4 5   6 7 8 9 0
q w e r t   y u i o p
a s d f g   h j k l ;
z x c v b   n m , . /

To the right of the letter & number keys:

(Low Case)   (Up Case)

- =   _ +

[ ] \   { } |

.   : "

                       < > ?